WOMEN IN THE WORLD OF CHINA

WOMEN'S ISSUES:
GLOBAL TRENDS

Women in the Arab World

Women in the World of Japan

Women in the World of Africa

Women in the World of China

Native Women in the Americas

Women in the World of India

Women in the Eastern European World

Women in the World of Southeast Asia

Women in the Hispanic World

Women in the World of Russia

Women in the Mediterranean World

Women in North America's Religious World

WOMEN'S ISSUES:
GLOBAL TRENDS

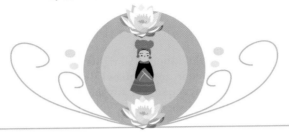

WOMEN IN THE WORLD OF CHINA

BY
ELLYN SANNA

Mason Crest Publishers
Philadelphia

Mason Crest Publishers Inc.
370 Reed Road
Broomall, Pennsylvania 19008
(866) MCP-BOOK (toll free)

First printing.
1 2 3 4 5 6 7 8 9 10

Library of Congress Cataloging-in-Publication Data

Sanna, Ellyn, 1958–
  Women in the world of China / by Ellyn Sanna.
    p. cm. — (Women's issues, global trends)
  Includes index.
  ISBN 1-59084-863-2   ISBN 1-59084-856-X (series)
  1. Sex role—China. 2. Women—China—Social conditions. I. Title. II. Series.
  HQ1075.5.C6S25 2005
  305.42'0951—dc22
                    2004014589

Interior design by Michelle Bouch and MK Bassett-Harvey.
Illustrations by Michelle Bouch.
Produced by Harding House Publishing Service, Inc.
Cover design by Benjamin Stewart.
Printed in India.

CONTENTS

INTRODUCTION

by Mary Jo Dudley

The last thirty years have been a time of great progress for women around the world. In some countries, especially where women have more access to education and work opportunities, the relationships between women and men have changed radically. The boundaries between men's roles and women's roles have been crossed, and women are enjoying many experiences that were denied them in past centuries.

But there is still much to be done. On the global stage, women are increasingly the ones who suffer most from poverty. At the same time that they produce 75 to 90 percent of the world's food crops, they are also responsible for taking care of their households. According to the United Nations, in no country in the world do men come anywhere near to spending as much time on housework as women do. This means that women's job opportunities are often extremely limited, contributing to the "feminization of poverty."

In fact, two out of every three poor adults are women. According to the Decade of Women, "Women do two-thirds of the world's work, receive 10 percent of the world's income, and own one percent of the means of production." Women often have no choice but to take jobs that lack long-term secu-

rity or adequate pay; many women work in dangerous working conditions or in unprotected home-based industries. This series clearly illustrates how historic events and contemporary trends (such as war, conflicts, and migration) have also contributed to women's loss of property and diminished access to resources.

A recent report from Human Rights Watch indicates that many countries continue to deny women basic legal protections. Amnesty International points out, "Governments are not living up to their promises under the Women's Convention to protect women from discrimination and violence such as rape and female genital mutilation." Many nations—including the United States—have not ratified the United Nations' Women's Treaty.

During times of armed conflict, especially under policies of ethnic cleansing, women are particularly at risk. Murder, torture, systematic rape, forced pregnancy and forced abortions are all too common human rights violations endured by women around the world. This series presents the experience of women in Vietnam, Cambodia, the Middle East, and other war torn regions.

In the political arena, equality between men and women has still not been achieved. Around the world, women are underrepresented in their local and national governments; on average, women represent only 10 percent of all legislators worldwide. This series provides excellent examples of key female leaders who have promoted women's rights and occupied unique leadership positions, despite historical contexts that would normally have shut them out from political and social prominence.

The Fourth World Conference on Women called upon the international community to take action in the following areas of concern:

- the persistent and increasing burden of poverty on women
- inequalities and inadequacies in access to education and training
- inequalities and inadequacies in access to health care and related services
- violence against women

- the effects of armed or other kinds of conflict on women
- inequality in economic structures and policies, in all forms of productive processes, and in access to resources
- insufficient mechanisms at all levels to promote the advancement of women
- lack of protection of women's human rights
- stereotyping of women and inequality in women's participation in all community systems, especially the media
- gender inequalities in the management of natural resources and the safeguarding of the environment
- persistent discrimination against and violation of the rights of female children

The Conference's mission statement includes these sentences: "Equality between women and men is a matter of human rights and a condition for social justice and is also a necessary and fundamental prerequisite for equality, development and peace. . . equality between women and men is a condition . . . for society to meet the challenges of the twenty-first century." This series provides examples of how women have risen above adversity, despite their disadvantaged social, economic, and political positions.

Each book in WOMEN'S ISSUES: GLOBAL TRENDS takes a look at women's lives in a different key region or culture, revealing the history, contributions, triumphs, and challenges of women around the world. Women play key roles in shaping families, spirituality, and societies. By interweaving historic backdrops with the modern-day evolving role of women in the home and in society at large, this series presents the important part women play as cultural communicators. Protection of women's rights is an integral part of universal human rights, peace, and economic security. As a result, readers who gain understanding of women's lives around the world will have deeper insight into the current condition of global interactions.

"NOODLES ARE NOT REAL FOOD; WOMEN ARE NOT REAL HUMAN BEINGS." —CHINESE PROVERB

HUMAN BEINGS WITH NO VALUE: THE HISTORICAL ROLE OF CHINESE WOMEN

When Yin-Lo was five years old, her grandmother broke her toes.

The week before, Yin-Lo had watched her grandmother weave a piece of white fabric. Now the cloth was a little more than a yard long (about a meter). Her grandmother took the material from the loom and carefully cut it into strips.

"Come here," her grandmother said. "Sit down beside me."

Yin-Lo knew her grandmother loved her—and even more important, she knew she had to obey her elders. But Yin-Lo knew what was coming next, and she was frightened. Trembling, she took a seat beside her grandmother.

The old woman removed her granddaughter's shoes. She held one of Yin-Lo's small feet in her gnarled fingers, and then she pushed all the toes backward except for the big toe. At first, Yin-Lo's foot only felt uncomfortable, but then her grandmother began to wrap the strips of white cloth tighter and tighter around Yin-Lo's foot, pressing the toes back so that they were folded under her sole. Her toes ached, and she whimpered.

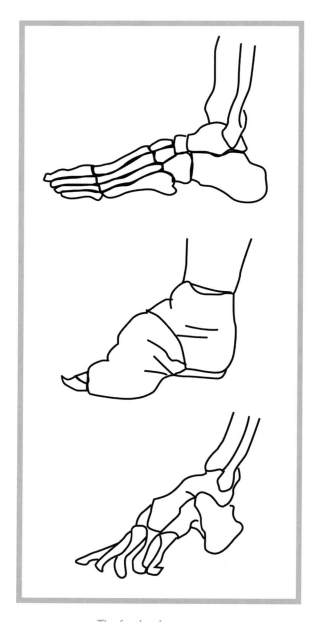

The footbinding process.

Her grandmother was always kind to Yin-Lo, but now she paid no attention to the little girl's pain. Around and around, she wrapped the strips of cloth, until Yin-Lo's foot looked like a tight little bundle of rags. Then her grandmother picked up Yin-Lo's other foot.

"If you are lucky," she said when she had finished wrapping all the strips of cloth, "you will have lotus of gold feet. Like me." She pointed down at her three-inch long feet (about 7.5 centimeters long). "At the very least you will have silver feet like your mother." Yin-Lo's grandmother held her fingers about four inches apart (about 10 centimeters). "No one in our family has big iron feet."

Yin-Lo sat for a moment looking at her feet. She knew when she grew up, she would have tiny feet that fit into pretty shoes like those her mother and grandmother wore. Men would admire her feet, and one day her husband would love her more if she could achieve lotus of gold feet.

But right now her feet ached.

As the weeks went by, Yin-Lo's feet hurt more and more. Each day her mother and grandmother sent her outside to push a big rock around and around the yard, around and around, again and again, until she wore a hollowed-out path in the earth. "Each step will help shape your foot into a tiny, perfect cone," her mother said, patting the tears off Yin-Lo's face. "It will make the binding go faster."

Yin-Lo tried to imagine the beautiful red shoes she would wear one day. But each step she took was torture.

Her grandmother would not listen to her cries of pain, and even her mother turned her head away. "It hurts now," she said, "but one day you will be glad. Men do not marry women with big feet."

Yin-Lo's toes felt as though they were on fire. She did not know it, but by now, the tiny bones had all broken. "I'd rather never marry," she muttered.

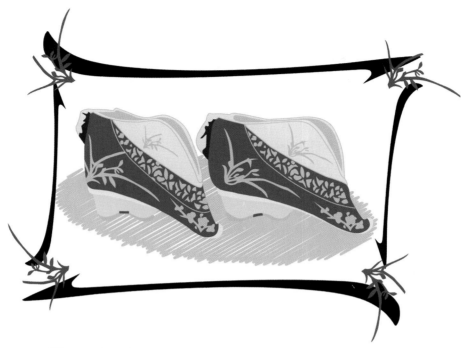

Women whose feet had been bound could wear tiny shoes like these.

Her grandmother pressed her lips tight. "A woman who does not marry is nothing."

"A husband will give you sons," Yin-Lo's mother added.

"And when you die, your children will tend your grave," the old woman finished.

Yin-Lo sighed and bit back the pain that pressed at her lips, trying to come out. She hobbled in another circle around the yard, pushing the heavy stone with her broken toes.

Footbinding began in China sometime in the tenth century. Although it may have been rare in the tenth, eleventh, and twelfth centuries, by the thirteenth

century it was common practice, a practice that endured into the twentieth century. Chinese poets associated bound feet with exquisite beauty. They wrote with wonder of the "slender arcs" small enough to fit in the palm of a man's hand, "moons forever new." Chinese men considered tiny feminine feet to be not only beautiful but erotic; in other words, they were a sexual turn-on.

Many cultures have practices that look strange from those looking in from the outside. For instance, in North America, many women squeeze their feet into tiny pointed shoes that elevate their heels on slender spikes, despite the fact that few women have triangular toes shaped like little elves' feet. In the eighteenth and nineteenth centuries, fashionable women squeezed their waists inside tight corsets; their ribs were compressed so much they could hardly breathe and they often "swooned," but their slender, wasp-like waists conformed to the beauty standards of their day. Styles such as these, like Chinese footbinding, *accentuate* the differences between men and women.

They also serve to restrict women, making them less able to compete in the

Fashionable nineteenth-century women in Europe and North America wore tight corsets to make their waists unnaturally slender.

Chinese women were often portrayed with their feet hidden.

WOMEN IN THE WORLD OF CHINA

male world of physical strength. High-heeled shoes affect the way a woman walks and limit her ability to run; a tight corset impaired a woman's breathing, so she had little energy for strenuous activity; but footbinding went still further. It permanently altered a woman's body. Today, many North American women go through cosmetic surgery, inserting silicon implants in their breasts and sucking fat cells from their thighs—but these body alterations still do not affect a woman's entire physical being as much as footbinding did. Footbinding permanently changed the very nature of a woman's identity.

A woman who wears high heels to work or for dressy occasions can kick them off when she gets home—but a woman whose feet were bound could never walk normally. She was forced to sit rather than stand; she had to stay at home, inside her house, rather than go out into the world. Because she exercised less, she was smaller, softer, weaker, less energetic. Meanwhile, by comparison, the men in her life appeared larger, more muscular, harder, and more active. Women were languid, delicate, and submissive; men were energetic, strong, and dominant.

Clearly, Chinese men were attracted to women with bound feet. And Chinese women *internalized* this standard of beauty. They shared men's perception that tiny feet were beautiful. They took pride in their useless, broken feet, and loving mothers inflicted the practice on their daughters. After all, a good mother wants what is best for her children—and what could be better for a daughter than that she be attractive enough to win a husband?

Chinese traditions also called for strict separation between the sexes. Men and women spent most of their time apart from one another, and when they had to be together, physical contact was avoided. Men lived "outside" lives, while women were confined to the "inner" world. *The Book of Rites*, an ancient book on ethics, summarized this outlook:

> In housing there should be a strict *demarcation* between the inner and outer parts, with a door separating them. The two parts should share nei-

ther a well, a washroom, nor a *privy*. The men are in charge of all affairs on the outside; the women manage the inside affairs. During the day, the men do not stay in their private rooms nor the women go beyond the inner door without good reason. . . . A girl ten or older does not go out, which means she remains permanently inside.

Such rigid divisions between the sexes required money; poor families could not afford to have two wells, two privies, or houses with inner and outer areas. As a result, these gender roles became associated with class distinctions. The wealthy, well-educated upper class kept their women invisible. But the belief that women were inferior seeped throughout all levels of Chinese culture. It was the foundation for the practice of footbinding—and then footbinding dug the belief even deeper into the realities of women's lives.

Almost all cultures around the globe have cultural practices that emphasize the differences between men and women. In China, these differences were extreme, creating a high wall around women's lives. Men were the ones who actively shaped society and ruled business and government; women did nothing worthwhile but produce sons. And meanwhile, footbinding kept a tight grip on both the minds and feet of Chinese women.

From 1644 until 1911, the Manchus who ruled China tried to prohibit the practice, but still it continued. Christian missionaries who came to China also tried to discourage footbinding, and in 1895, a group of European missionary women established the Natural Feet Society in Shanghai. Members promised not to bind the feet of their daughters or allow their sons to marry women with bound feet. The society spread through China, reaching thousands of people—but still footbinding persisted. Even when Chinese immigrants came to North America, they often brought the custom with them.

Through the centuries, not all Chinese men supported footbinding. As early as the thirteenth century, Ch'e Jo-shui wrote, "Little children not yet four or five . . . who have done nothing wrong, nevertheless are made to suffer unlimited

Concubines attend a long-ago Chinese emperor.

The first women to bind their feet may have been dancers. When footbinding was carried to an extreme, however, a woman's feet were too tiny and unstable for her to dance.

pain to bind [their feet] small. I do not know what use this is." In the nineteenth century, reformer Kang Youwei wrote to the Chinese emperor, "Foreigners laugh at us . . . and criticize us for being barbarians. . . . There is nothing which makes us objects of ridicule so much as footbinding." Early in the twentieth century, a male poet wrote these lines:

A girl's feet, yes, a daughter's feet—
A natural part of the body.
Be he a son, be she a daughter—
All born from the same mother.

The ten toes are like brothers,
Siblings living in harmony.
They wish for wholesome prosperity,
Sharing what heaven has endowed.

For what reason, ladies, may I ask:
When did this evil custom begin?
Why, be she young or old, rich or poor,
Shrink the feet to three inches?

A life in the inner chamber, a living hell,
In solitary confinement,
Beneath her hemline, bound into a tight bundle—
Layers upon layers of restriction.

Walking slowly, moving gingerly,
Ever fearful of toppling over.
Clogged circulation, congested respiration,
The pinching pain of pecking birds.

. . .

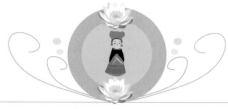

In China, opium had long been used to stop diarrhea—but in the seventeenth and eighteenth centuries, the Chinese began to use it recreationally. In its own version of America's "war on drugs," the imperial government outlawed the importation of opium. Despite this restriction, the opium trade continued to flourish. Merchants from many countries, including the United States, made huge profits from the growing number of Chinese addicts. These foreigners were annoyed by the attempts of Chinese authorities to stop the opium trade. In the spring of 1839, Chinese authorities at Canton confiscated and burned millions of pounds of opium. In response, the British occupied positions around Canton.

In the war that followed, the Chinese could not match the technological and tactical superiority of the British forces. In 1842, China agreed to the provisions of the Treaty of Nanking. Hong Kong was ceded to Great Britain, and other ports, including Canton, were opened to British residence and trade. The French and Americans approached the Chinese after the Nanking Treaty's provisions became known, and in 1844, they gained the same trading rights as the British. The advantages granted the three nations by the Chinese set a precedent that would dominate China's relations with the world for the next century. Meanwhile, the opium trade continued to thrive.

The Opium War was about far more than drug control; deep cultural conflicts between East and West motivated the war—and for the time being, the East lost. The Opium War was the beginning of the period Chinese refer to as the time of unequal treaties, an era of unprecedented degradation for China. The humiliation China suffered is still remembered, and the memory affects important aspects of China's foreign policy today.

Superior people set the trends;
They'll take the first step to loosen the bindings.
Now she can walk, attend school;
How can she not be happy?

Schools for boys, schools for girls—
An idea bright as candlelight.
An imperial edict, an order from the government;
There will be no going back to suffering.

As China moved into the twentieth century, the thoughts expressed in this poem gradually began to spread. This was a time of new ideas, and the world was changing. Although China had long held itself separate from other countries, it could not keep out the new thoughts that filtered into it from the West. In 1842, China had lost the *Opium War* to Great Britain, and for the next 150 years, many of the Chinese coastal cities came under the control of Britain and France. These were years of foreign *exploitation* for China—but Westerners also brought with them the winds of change to many Chinese traditions.

Even the government could not resist. For centuries, China had been an *imperial dynasty*, but in 1911, Sun Yat-sen toppled the emperor. For the first time, China became a *republic*. Soon, however, the country disintegrated into smaller districts, each ruled by a different warlord. A military general named Chiang Kai-shek united the country, only to lose the country to the *communists* in 1949.

A communist leader, Mao Tse-tung (or Zedong, as it is spelled in China), drove both foreigners and Chiang Kai-shek's followers out of the country and proclaimed the People's Republic. Under Mao's firm rule, footbinding at last disappeared.

"GENUINE
EQUALITY
BETWEEN
THE SEXES
CAN
ONLY BE
REALIZED
IN THE
PROCESS OF
THE
SOCIALIST
TRANSFOR-
MATION
OF SOCIETY
AS A
WHOLE."
—MAO
TSE-TUNG

2

WOMEN HOLD UP HALF THE SKY: WOMEN AND THE CULTURAL REVOLUTION

When Mao Tse-tung took over China in 1949, he proclaimed that the "Chinese people have finally stood up for themselves." In reality, Mao Tse-tung ruled a one-man *dictatorship*. He replaced China's traditional values and religions with nationalism—love of the "motherland."

Mao believed that all traces of Chinese traditional culture needed to be erased. He saw the Chinese as dominated by three separate institutions: the state, the clan and family, and the religious system. Women, for their part, were dominated by all three of these institutions and were also dominated by men. These "four authorities"—political authority, clan authority, *theocratic* authority, and the authority of the husband—had to be pulled down in order for China to become a truly *egalitarian* nation. In 1966, Mao instituted the Cultural Revolution. He intended to free China from the "four olds": habits, customs, *ideals*, and *creeds*.

Mao argued that the Chinese Revolution had become rigid and betrayed its basic principles. To reinvigorate it, he invited young people to join the Red Guards and attack what he called the *bourgeois* elements in society. Many of

Mao Tse-tung

WOMEN IN THE WORLD OF CHINA

As a youngster, Mao refused to go along with the arranged marriage his father had set up. He was later involved with radical groups that opposed traditional Chinese marriage customs. After he became China's dictator, he spoke often against the oppression of women, an oppression he believed could only be changed by communism. According to Mao, women hold up half the sky; in other words, they do their share in creating and maintaining the world.

China's brightest and most creative people were imprisoned for "incorrect" thoughts—such as liking Western music or believing in Confucianism (see chapter 3). Tens of thousands were killed for similar crimes, and many others had to abandon their jobs to work on *collective* farms. In the space of only a few years, China's ancient history and traditions were all but erased. Chinese society reeled under the blow, and chaos was often the result.

Mao Tse-tung often spoke of the important roles women would play in building Communist China—and in many ways, women's lives did improve.

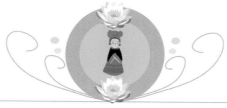

For a short period in the late sixties, Mao Tse-Tung's "Little Red Book" was one of the most studied books in the world. Assembled by Communist Party editors from Mao's speeches and writings, it was intended as a guide for those involved in the Cultural Revolution. By December 1967, there were already 350 million copies in print. People in China were forced to gather in study groups to spend hours discussing every line of the book so that they could apply them to their lives.

Here are a few of Mao's thoughts on women:

"Protect the interests of the youth, women and children—provide assistance to young students who cannot afford to continue their studies, help the youth and women to organize in order to participate on an equal footing in all work useful to the war effort and to social progress, ensure freedom of marriage and equality as between men and women, and give young people and children a useful education. . . ."

"[In agricultural production] our fundamental task is to adjust the use of labour power in an organized way and to encourage women to do farm work."

"Men and women must receive equal pay for equal work in production."

"With the completion of agricultural cooperation, many co-operatives are finding themselves short of labour. It has become necessary to arouse the great mass of women who did not work in the fields before to take their place on the labour front. . . . China's women are a vast reserve of labour power. This reserve should be tapped in the struggle to build a great socialist country."

"Enable every woman who can work to take her place on the labour front, under the principle of equal pay for equal work. This should be done as quickly as possible."

In modern China, Chairman Mao is still honored.

Communist propaganda posters portrayed women as strong and smiling.

WOMEN IN THE WORLD OF CHINA

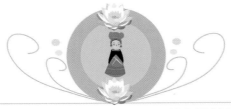

Xinran, the author of **The Good Women of China**, tells the story of a Chinese teacher who had lived for a time in India. During the Cultural Revolution, she maintained that the Mao suit was too mannish for her tastes, and so she wore a sari under her regulation jacket. The Red Guards condemned her for "worshipping and having blind faith in foreign things." Some of her own former students were the ones who mistreated her. They apologized, saying, "If we did not struggle against you, we would get into trouble and our families with us."

Another woman teacher told of receiving lipstick and high-heeled shoes as a gift from a distant relative in Indonesia. Knowing that foreign gifts could get her into trouble, she immediately threw them away—but a little girl found the items in the garbage and reported the teacher's "crime." For many months afterward, the teacher was driven through the streets in the back of a truck so that the crowds could abuse her for her sins.

Except for Mao's wife Jian Qing, however, who was very influential during the Cultural Revolution, women were generally kept in *subordinate* positions in the party leadership. They were encouraged to be "sexless," and romantic love and sexual attraction was condemned.

When Mao Tse-tung died in 1977, the Cultural Revolution was officially declared to have ended. But the effects of the Cultural Revolution continued to touch China's people. A generation of scientists, educated people, artists, and thinkers had been wiped out, leaving a society with huge gaps. The Red Guards

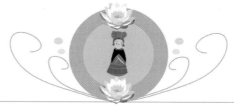

JIANG QING (1914–1991)

Jiang Qing (sometimes spelled Chiang Ch'ing) married Mao Tse-tung in 1939. She remained in the background of Chinese communist affairs until the outbreak of the Cultural Revolution in 1966, when she was appointed deputy director of the Cultural Revolution. In this role, she incited teenagers and young adults against senior party and government officials, and replaced nearly all earlier works of art with revolutionary Maoist works. She was one of the most powerful political figures during Mao's last years. For her role in the Cultural Revolution, she was arrested by her husband's successor and sentenced to death. Her sentence was later commuted to life imprisonment.

Jiang Qing

After the Communist Revolution in China, women could work alongside men as agricultural laborers.

had destroyed irreplaceable ancient buildings, artifacts, antiques, books, and paintings; Chinese traditional arts and ideas were buried deep beneath the years of Mao's rule. China's economy suffered as well, as did its educational system. As many as 100 million people had been killed.

Today, most people, both inside and outside China, view the Cultural Revolution as a disaster for all concerned. The cause and meaning of the revolution are *controversial*, however. Supporters of democracy and human rights *activists* tend to blame communism itself for the revolution's terrible failures. Meanwhile, the Communist Party blames these same failures on too much public participation in government rather than too little; according to this viewpoint, China must be governed by a strong party in which the public has only limited input.

Some Chinese *feminists* believe that Mao brought the first taste of equality to China's women. Under Mao, the roles between men and women became more blurred, as women went to work in the armed forces, in factories, on farms, and in various forms of public service. As a result, more women became financially independent, no longer totally reliant on their fathers, husbands, or sons for support.

But there was much work still to be done. Even in the midst of the Revolution, women continued to be treated as second-class creatures.

During the 1990s, Xinran author of *The Good Women of China*, hosted a radio call-in program for women. She gave women across China the chance to tell their stories. One woman called in to tell the story of her life during the Cultural Revolution.

I was very happy when I first arrived at the area liberated by the Party. Everything was so new and strange: in the fields, peasants and soldiers were indistinguishable. . . . Men and women wore the same clothes and did the same things; the leaders were not distinguishable by symbols of rank. Everyone was talking about the future of China; every day there

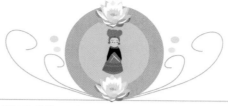

In the cities, small "street factories" were set up to allow women to work part-time and bring their children to work with them. Many of these small factories grew into larger collectively owned and run factories, employing hundreds of workers and producing all kinds of goods. In Beijing, 180,000 women were involved in setting up more than 400 street factories and 2,900 street production units.

Older factories got rid of bonuses and incentives (giving workers more pay for more and better work), which tended to favor men who were stronger and more free to work overtime. And while differences in wages still remained, big efforts were made to "bring the bottom up" increasing benefits and wages of workers in the lowest paying jobs, where women were still concentrated.

The flag of the People's Republic of China.

were criticisms and condemnations of the old system. . . . The female students were treated like princesses, valued for the lightness of spirit and beauty we brought.

In the midst of all this excitement, the young woman was singled out by the regimental leader. "Are you prepared to complete any mission the Party gives you?" he asked her.

Many statues of Mao continue to look down over modern China.

"Of course!" she replied.

She was taken to a senior office who looked her up and down. "Not bad," he said, "not bad at all. From today you are my secretary."

That night the senior officer informed her what her "mission" really was: she was to become his wife. The next day the Party celebrated their marriage, and the woman remained married to the man for the next forty years. Recently, he said to her that she was like a faded gray cloth, not good enough to make trousers from, not good enough to cover a bed or even to be used as a dishcloth. "All I am good for," the woman told Xinran, "is wiping mud off his feet. To him, my only function is to serve . . . so he can move on to higher office."

Xinran's story shows that the old ways of thinking lingered on, even during the Cultural Revolution. Despite Mao's egalitarian ideals, he failed on many counts. He did not eradicate the prejudice against women. He failed to bring them true equality. As powerful as Mao was, he could not totally erase centuries of tradition from the Chinese mind. Even today, Confucius has a firmer hold on Chinese thinking than does the Communist Party.

"THE HUSBAND IS HEAVEN; THE WIFE IS EARTH. . . . HEAVEN IS HONORED . . . EARTH IS LOWLY."
—TWELFTH-CENTURY CONFUCIAN CLASSIC

OBEDIENT AND LOWLY:
CHINESE PHILOSOPHY AND WOMEN

Long ago, five hundred years before the birth of Christ, a woman gave birth to a little boy in the village of Zou in the Chinese state of Lu. Her husband died when the child was three, and so she raised her son alone. Their family was poor but noble, and the woman must have trained her son well. In any case, he grew up with a reputation for fairness, politeness, and a love of learning. He came to be called Confucius. The world remembers his name; it never knew his mother's.

As a young adult, Confucius apparently forgot about the woman who had given birth to him. He was busy with his own life, traveling throughout China and studying at the imperial capital, Zhou, where he spoke with the great male thinkers of his day. When he went back home to Lu, he shared his wisdom with other men and became famous as a teacher. His mother plays no part in his story, nor does any woman, although Confucius did marry and have children.

Confucius apparently didn't think much of women. After all, his life was busy with exciting male doings. He was fussy and demanding when it came to

the food his wife served him, and after a while, she left him. Perhaps his unhappy marriage helped shape his beliefs about women.

The years went by peacefully enough until Confucius was thirty-five; then his land was overtaken by conflict, and its leader, Duke Zhao, was forced to flee. Confucius followed him. At first, Duke Zhao came frequently to Confucius for advice, and the duke considered granting Confucius his own land. One of the duke's advisors, however, counseled him against Confucius, and the duke stopped seeking Confucius's counsel. When other nobles began plotting against Confucius's position, Duke Zhao refused to protect him. At last, Confucius returned to Lu.

But conditions there were no better than before, and Confucius retired from public life to concentrate on teaching and studying. In his fifties, however, he was made a city magistrate by the new Duke of Lu, and under his administration the city flourished; he was promoted several times, eventually becoming Grand Secretary of Justice and then Chief Minister of Lu.

Neighboring countries began to worry that Lu would become too powerful, and they sent messengers with gifts and dancers to distract the duke during a holiday. When the duke abandoned his duties to receive the messengers—and their gifts—Confucius threw up his hands and left the country.

For the next five years, Confucius wandered around China with his disciples, the young men who followed him. He studied the character of each of his disciples and taught them all how to think and find answers for themselves. His many conversations with his students were written down in a book called *The Analects*. Meanwhile, he found that his presence at royal courts was rarely tolerated for long before nobles would begin plotting to drive him out or have him killed. He eventually returned to Lu, where he spent the rest of his years quietly teaching and writing. He died of old age at seventy-two.

Something about Confucius obviously had the power to upset the *status quo*; otherwise, officials and nobles throughout long-ago China would not have

Confucius

Confucius as an old man.

hated this man so much. Despite his lack of any permanent success, either financially or politically, his name has never been erased from history. Most of us today, even if we aren't Chinese, connect the name Confucius with wisdom, and his teachings still have great insights to offer the world. These insights are not religious thoughts concerned with the supernatural world or the life hereafter; instead, they address everyday human life. During his lifetime, Confucius sought to bring order and harmony to his society. After his death, his teachings were welcomed by China's imperial rulers because Confucian thought reinforced the power and role of the emperor.

CONFUCIAN-INSPIRED CHINESE PROVERBS

A women's duty is not to control or take charge.

Women's greatest duty is to produce a son.

A woman ruler is like a hen crowing.

We should not be too familiar with the lower orders or with women.

The woman with no talent is the one who has merit.

Women are to be led and to follow others.

Women cannot be taught and cannot be instructed.

Unfortunately, his dialogues with his students were full of his poor opinion of women. For instance, he spoke of the "ideal person," who could only be male, never female. He declared that "only uneducated women were virtuous." According to Confucian thought, a stable society is built on five relationships: between rule and advisor; between father and son; between husband and wife; between older brother and younger brother; and between friend and friend. Only the relationship between friends was considered to be between equals. All the others were based on a superior-inferior relationship. "Between husbands and wives," he taught, "there should be attention to their separate functions." This meant that men were the breadwinners who worked outside the house and made money. Women were in essence the men's servants; they had no money, no income, and no rights.

What's more, according to Confucian teaching, a man could have more than one wife; he was also free to divorce his wife and remarry. A woman, on the other hand, was expected to be completely loyal to her husband, even after he died. Her entire life was built around obedience to male authority: when she was young, she obeyed her father; when she became an adult, she married and obeyed her husband; and if, when she became an old woman, her husband died before she did, she then obeyed her son.

Confucian ideas stressed the importance of men and women doing things differently, to underline their essential difference from one another. Rituals were built around small, daily events. For example, when greeting his parents in the morning, a man should say, "At your service," while his wife should always say, "Bless you." When participating in a ceremony, men were to bow two times, while a woman bowed four times.

Much of Confucius's ideas about men and women were built on the concept of yin and yang. According to this way of looking at the world, yin and yang are the two complimentary forces that shape reality. Yin is dark, passive, and female, while yang is bright, assertive, and male. Yin-yang is often represented by

The yin-yang.

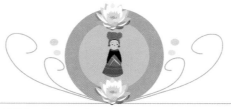

Confucianism is not the only philosophy that has shaped Chinese culture. The teachings of Buddha, the Indian teacher, also played a role—and women's position in Buddhism was far more positive. Although Buddha lived in a culture that saw women as inferior, just as ancient Chinese culture did, he believed that women could prove themselves as spiritually developed as men. Kuan Yin (also spelled Kwan Yin or Quan Yin), a Buddhist goddess, is one of the most popular deities in all of Asia. Her name in Chinese roughly translates as "the One who Hears the Cries of the World."

Taoism is another philosophy that has played a role in Chinese thought. Founded by Lao Tzu in the sixth century B.C.E., Taoism teaches that happiness and peaceful coexistence can be achieved by following the Tao, also known as the Way. The Tao is a concept that cannot be fully understood; it is the mysterious way of nature that is inherently female, acting as a mother to all things. Therefore, women should be treated with reverence and respect. The female body is seen as beautiful and sacred, and women are equal with men for all ranks but the highest of Divine Lord. Taoists worshiped many goddesses, including the Queen Mother of the West, who could grant immortality.

The development of a feminine religion in the heart of male-oriented China is amazing. But Taoism was often viewed with suspicion and given little credit in Chinese histories. As Confucianism grabbed hold through the centuries, its more conservative values took away much of the sexual freedom experienced by Taoist women.

A Chinese Buddhist temple.

two fish in a circle: one fish is black with a white dot in it; the other is white with a black dot. Yin cannot exist without yang, nor can yang exist without yin. Without day there could not be night—but without night, we would not have day. Inside every yin is a little bit of yang—and vice versa. All things are inter-related and interdependent. Each is shaped by the other.

These ideas seem to support the equality of the sexes, and they make good sense. After all, men have some feminine qualities, just as women have some masculine qualities. And the two sexes depend on one another, each influenc-ing the other's lives. But in Confucian thought, yang is considered superior to yin. According to one ancient book, "Yang on the top and yin on the bottom is proper for honored and lowly; thus male and female are proper and attain their

Kuan Yin, the Buddhist goddess of mercy.

place." Men acted with their wills, women with their feelings. Men initiated actions, women merely endured. Men lived outside lives, women were hidden away on the inside. "Therefore wives take as their virtues gentleness and compliance and do not excel through strength or intellectual discrimination."

According to Adeline Yen Mah, author of *Watching the Tree*, even today, every Chinese person wears a Confucian thinking cap. No matter how modern she may be, her thoughts are unconsciously shaped by centuries of Confucian beliefs. Just as footbinding once bound women's feet, Confucius's teachings have quietly and surely bound women's lives for centuries.

"A WIFE MARRIED IS LIKE A PONY BOUGHT; I'LL RIDE HER AND WHIP HER AS I LIKE."
—CHINESE PROVERB

4

DAUGHTER, WIFE, AND MOTHER: WOMEN'S ROLES IN CHINESE FAMILIES

Lung Feng had only been married for a month when her husband Chin decided to travel to another region looking for work. He left Feng behind. After all, his mother needed someone to help her.

Feng and her mother-in-law were not close. In fact, they were more like servant and mistress. Feng's mother-in-law insisted that Feng get up at three every morning to wash the family's rice, and then she had to pound and grind the rice all through the day's long hot hours until she was exhausted. No matter what Feng did, she could never please her mother-in-law. From morning to night, her mother-in-law scolded her. Feng longed for her husband to return.

But when Chin at last came home, his mother told him Feng had been looking for a lover while he was gone. "Beat her until she is black and blue," his mother insisted. "Beat her until the welts rise on her back." Chin didn't meet his wife's eyes as he obeyed his mother. After all, a son should obey his parents.

One day, Feng's brother came to visit while Chin was beating her. Feng looked at her brother, her eyes full of pleading. Surely, he would help her. But

In rural areas, Chinese women's lives are still filled with strenuous physical labor.

WOMEN IN THE WORLD OF CHINA

her brother only hung his head. "I have no face," he muttered as he left; he meant he was too humiliated to watch.

Feng's life had become a long, endurance test of endless hard labor and brutal beatings. She knew there was no way out. Her only hope was that one day she would bear a son. Eventually, her son would grow up and take a wife. By then Chin's mother would be dead—and Feng would be the mother-in-law. It would be her turn to rule her daughter-in-law. It was the only power she would ever have.

This story could describe the lives of many Chinese women who lived any time during the past eight centuries. Only later in the twentieth century have things begun to change. Older women today still remember the narrow lives they lived as young women.

CHINESE PROVERBS

A new bride must be the first to work and the last to eat.

A good daughter-in-law is never thirsty, never hungry, never sleepy, never tired, and never has to go to the toilet.

Mothers-in-law beating daughters-in-law is justified everywhere.

A woman dressed in traditional Chinese clothing.

The original Chinese word for "wife"—*fu*—meant "daughter-in-law" as much as "wife." The word came from other terms that meant "support" and "submit." In other words, a wife was someone who "submitted," both to her husband and to her mother-in-law. When she married, she lost any individuality she had ever had; her entire identity was now absorbed into her husband's family.

In chapter 3, we spoke of the importance of relationships in Confucian thinking. The parent-child relationship was one of the cornerstones that kept Chinese society stable. Today, filial piety—a term that means the respect and honor children owe their parents—continues to be the foundation of traditional Chinese families. A child's life and body are gifts from her parents. She can do nothing in her life that would bring dishonor to them.

In the past, many children memorized twenty-four *classical* examples of filial piety. These included:

- the perfect filial child who would lie in his parents' bed to warm it for them in the wintertime, and to allow the mosquitoes to eat their fill in the summer.
- the filial adult who would dress up in baby clothes on his fiftieth birthday and dance for his parents, so they might feel light and youthful.
- the filial child who cried when his sick mother wanted bamboo shoots in the dead of winter; he wept so sincerely that his tears became the soft rains of spring and bamboo shoots burst through the snow.

These examples may seem silly for those of us who are on the outside looking in on traditional Chinese culture, but aspects of our culture may seem equally foolish to outsiders. For those who grew up immersed in Chinese culture, respect for parents shaped their entire lives—and if you were a girl, sub-

missiveness and obedience was the guiding light of your entire existence. You would never enter your father's presence without asking his permission first, and you never left your father without his saying you could go. Unless you were spoken to first, you never spoke to your father. If you were scolded, you bowed your head and thanked your father for his correction. A son would grow up to have a job and lead a busy life in the outside world—but a daughter would leave her father's house only to go to her husband's.

Unlike Chin, Feng's husband, Zhou's husband was a rich man. But this did not mean that Zhou's life was less restricted than Feng's. Zhou spent her life sewing buttons onto factory overalls.

When Zhou was middle-aged, an American visitor asked her why she worked so hard when her husband was a wealthy man. Zhou opened her eyes wide. "Do you want me to go crazy? How could I sit here in my husband's house every day, exactly as I have sat for the last twenty-seven years, thinking the same thoughts, seeing the same things as I have done every day since I married, and not do anything? From the time I was ten years old, I was shut in my father's house. I was excited to marry and leave his house—but I have been in this house for the last twenty-seven years. I have never left except for two times when I attended funerals. Don't take from me my only way of passing time."

Zhou did not know how to read. She could not have friends over to talk and laugh. Her children were all daughters, and they were grown and living with their husbands' families. Her life was empty and barren, while her husband came and went as he pleased. Zhou knew there were other women in his life, and sometimes she felt jealous and lonely.

And yet Zhou told her visitor how much she loved her husband. "He provides for me and does not reproach me for my lack of sons. He is kind and indulgent." She sighed. "It's just that I am so tired of being treated like a child."

Traditional Chinese women are expected to be respectful and submissive.

In Chiina, extended families may all live in one household. Most families have fewer children than this one does.

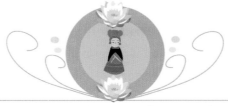

- Families in China usually included many generations living together, often under the same roof. The oldest male was usually in charge of everyone in the house.

- Chinese families had little sense of **individualism**. Decisions were made that benefited the entire family, and family honor and family achievements were more important than individual needs or achievements.

- For Chinese families, the family name (what most Westerners consider the last name) comes first. Then the individual name (Westerners' first name) follows. For example, if your name were Ron Brown, in China, it would be Brown Ron.

- Because men were considered superior to women, they kept their family names and carried on the family history. Grandfathers, fathers, uncles, and sons were more important than grandmothers, mothers, aunts, and daughters.

- Sons learned their family's trade, and daughters learned to manage a household.

- A father decided who his children married.

- Poor families sometimes sold their daughters to be servants of the rich.

- Only sons could go to school, and only a son could inherit property.

Chinese married men have always had far more freedom than their wives—socially, financially, and sexually. Men were not expected be faithful to their wives; they could take a second wife, divorce, or have a *concubine*. A totally different standard applied to women, though. The stability of the Chinese family depended on wives and mothers knowing their place.

Modern trends, however, are *eroding* this traditional stability. One of these trends is the growing divorce rate. Many Chinese shake their heads at this development, while others see it as a hopeful sign that women are no longer as oppressed as they once were.

Today, the Chinese divorce rate is 10.4 percent, far lower than in the United States, where around half of all marriages end in divorce. Still, the Chinese rate is much higher than it once was. According to Pi Xiaoming, a Beijing divorce lawyer, "Only a few years ago, people would let a temple be destroyed before they would let a marriage fail." Now divorce is a far more acceptable alternative. Women initiate more than 70 percent of Chinese divorces—and the reason they most often give for wanting a divorce is their husband's unfaithfulness. Chinese women are no longer willing to put up with the traditional double standards.

More and more Chinese women also want romance and affection from their husbands. "My husband never kissed me, not once," said one divorced woman. "We had a child, but he never kissed me." Another newlywed woman wrote to Xinran, author of *The Good Women of China*, "Never think of a man as a tree whose shade you can rest in. Women are just fertilizer, rotting away to make men strong. . . . There is no real love." Women like these are frustrated and resentful. They feel they deserve something better.

Not all Chinese men are happy with this new way of thinking. "Chinese men need other women," said a thirty-two-year-old man from Shanghai. "Family

WOMEN IN THE WORLD OF CHINA

Some Modern Chinese women are changing their expectations of marriage.

WOMEN IN THE WORLD OF CHINA

life is one thing; life outside is another. You don't have to hide it; everyone at work knows who my girlfriend is." You can hear the echo of centuries of Chinese tradition in his words.

Some of those same traditions encourage modern Chinese men in the belief that beating their wives is acceptable behavior. According to the Chinese Academy of Social Sciences, domestic violence occurs in at least 30 percent of mainland China's families. Guo Jianmei, director of the Centre for Women's Law Studies and Legal Services, believes the percentage is actually far higher, since many victims never report beatings for fear of bringing disgrace to their families. "Abused women often believe the batterings are a normal part of married life," says Guo Jianmei, "or blame themselves for having done something wrong to trigger the violence." Family members discourage these women from coming forward with their stories. After all, a well-known ancient proverb states: "A wife married is like a pony bought; I'll ride her and whip her as I like." A woman is still little more than an animal in the minds of many Chinese families.

A program called Domestic Violence: Research, Intervention, and Prevention in China is trying to change this centuries-old way of thinking. The program educates medical professionals to help them identify abuse, assist victims, and bring perpetrators to justice. One doctor in the program reports the story of a woman who was dragged from her bed by her husband, thrown on the floor, and beaten—all because she refused to have an abortion. "He wants a son," the woman told the doctor. "But his brother's wife told him I'm having a baby girl. So he tried to force me to abort the child."

In the past, a doctor would have treated this woman, but he would have dismissed her story as a private matter between husband and wife. Today, new medical policies are working to break the cycle of abuse. Domestic abuse is a growing issue in Western nations, and attention to this family tragedy has finally seeped into Chinese society as well. As more and more professionals are

educated in the West or are exposed to Western movies, novels, and other media sources, new ways of thinking gradually gain ground.

And yet the prejudice against women remains ingrained in the fabric of Chinese life. Many feminists worry that China's one-child policy is yet another move that hurts girls' positions within the family.

Around 1980, when the Chinese government began to worry that uncontrolled population growth would lead to uncontrolled poverty, it imposed a strict limit on the number of children a couple could have: only one. Though the policy isn't always completely enforced, by 2001, China's total fertility rate had dropped from 5.8 children per woman in 1978 to only 1.8 children per woman.

A woman who has had a child must have an *IUD* inserted; a woman who gives birth to a second child must be *sterilized*. This policy is usually enforced regardless of risk factors, side effects, or medical history. In most cases, this

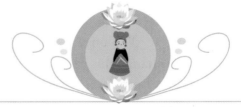

MORE THAN ONE PERSPECTIVE

Not everyone agrees that the one-child policy is bad for women. Some feminists believe that the policy frees women from the ongoing responsibility to bear children. With far smaller families, women have more opportunities to pursue a career. They are not limited to motherhood as their only role in life.

This billboard in China encourages the one-child policy.

Chinese respect the elderly.

means that women have only one chance to give birth to the son that will guarantee her approval from her husband, from her family, and from society. Although sex-selective abortion is technically illegal, it is still a common practice, as is *infanticide*. Little girls are not valued in many Chinese families.

Still, there is much that is valuable in Chinese family traditions. For example, Westerners could learn from the respect and reverence with which Chinese adults treat their elderly parents. Older adults are often valued members of a family who all live under one roof; the elderly contribute their insight and wisdom to the younger members of the family.

Traditionally, the family has always been the most important unit of Chinese society, and for the most part, this is true today as well. In rural areas, three or four generations are still likely to live in one household. In urban areas, families tend to be smaller. Often, both parents work, and women's and men's roles are not so very different from one another. Despite these changes, family ties continue to be a major force in the lives of many Chinese women.

As modern Chinese women develop a greater sense of their own identities, they can redefine the traditional roles of daughter, wife, and mother. Perhaps they will use as their role models women from China's own past, for not every Chinese woman was meek and submissive; China has a rich history, sprinkled with stories of strong women. Hopefully, modern Chinese women will one day be able to abandon the restrictions of the past while at the same time draw strength from the heritage of courage left behind by these long-ago women who dared to prove their worth.

"A MARE IS
NOT FIT TO
GO INTO
BATTLE—
AND A
WOMAN
CANNOT
TAKE A
MAN'S
PLACE."
—CHINESE
PROVERB

5

WARRIORS, EMPRESSES, AND CONCUBINES: CHINESE WOMEN WHO PROVED WOMEN'S WORTH

Long, long ago, a young girl named Mulan went to the market to buy a horse. She needed the horse because the Huns were invading her land. These nomads, who came from what is now Turkey, *looted* Chinese settlements for grain and other goods. Mulan was skilled in the martial arts—and she knew that her father was too old to fight, while her brother was too young. She dressed herself in her brother's clothes, said good-bye to her family, and rode off to war.

Mulan was a brave and skillful warrior. She distinguished herself in battle and was often promoted, until at last she became a general who was known for brilliant military strategy. All through her twelve-year military career, however, no one ever discovered she was a woman.

When the war was over at last, all the ranking officers were honored in person by the emperor. When Mulan's turn came to be presented to the emperor, he asked what Mulan would like as "his" reward for bravery and military skill. Mulan replied that the only thing she wanted was another horse—one that would take her quickly to her family. The emperor granted the request, and Mulan went home, back to a woman's life of weaving and housekeeping.

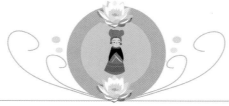

Today, not only Chinese children know the story of Mulan. Thanks to Disney's movie, children all over the world can identify with this young girl's courage and strength.

However, some critics have pointed to major discrepancies between Disney's Mulan and the original story:

- The Disney movie portrays Mulan as a bumbling private who never gains enough skill to be promoted, when in fact, she was a twelve-year veteran who retired as a general.
- Disney's Mulan is unskilled when she sets off for war, rather than an accomplished martial artist.
- The Huns in Disney's movie are portrayed as Mongols rather than Turks.
- Disney's Mulan hugs the emperor and kisses the dragon, acting more like a Western girl who is conforming to male expectations. Traditionally, Chinese people do not hug and kiss in public and Mulan would certainly not have wanted to give the emperor any ideas!

Mulan

Wu Zetian

Did she settle comfortably into her old life? Or did she often dream of the days when she was respected as a strong and competent man? According to some versions of the legend, the emperor eventually heard a rumor that Mulan was a woman, and he pressured her to become his concubine. When the emperor would not take no for an answer, Mulan could see no way to continue living her life by her own terms. Nevertheless, she found a way to escape from the emperor's clutches: she drew her sword and took her own life.

Mulan's story has been told to generation after generation of Chinese children. In the long centuries when women's lives were confined and hidden, the story of Mulan must have offered young girls a wonderful fantasy, a sense of what "might have been," if only their lives were different.

Stories like Mulan's demonstrate that Chinese women have a long heritage of strength and courage. Although they have endured centuries of oppression, through the ages, brave women like Mulan stood up for themselves so assertively that their stories still endure. One of the earliest of these outstanding women is Wu Zetian, the only female monarch in the two-thousand-year period from 221 B.C.E. to A.D. 1911.

Wu Zetian was intelligent, charming, and utterly determined. She entered the palace as a concubine when she was only fourteen, but she worked hard to improve her lot. For twelve years, she served as the emperor's secretary, proving her education and intelligence, but the emperor never promoted her. Neither did she give birth to his child. The emperor's son, however, fell in love with Wu Zetian, and when his father died, he married her, making her empress.

Wu Zetian's husband was often sick, and so she became the actual ruler of China. When her husband died, she was able to stabilize the political situation and keep the throne. Under her rule, China was prosperous and peaceful. She encouraged and supported other women who rose to prominent positions in both politics and the arts, and she was known for her power, wisdom, and achievement.

When Wu Zetian died, she left orders that a blank tablet should be erected in front of her tomb. She did not want to leave an *epitaph* telling the world who she had been and what she had accomplished, for she knew there were two sides to the story. On the one hand, she had been a successful ruler—but she had sacrificed everything for her position, including family, friends, and love. Even today, the Chinese have conflicting opinions about Wu Zetian. She is often called "the iron-hand empress"—but whether that is an insult or a compliment varies from person to person. Wu Zetian dared to break the rules that governed women. Did that make her stronger than other women—or did it make her an *egomaniac* who had to have her own way?

In any case, Wu Zetian was not the only Chinese woman who dared to break free from the traditional restrictions on women's lives. Wang Zhaojun is another long-ago Chinese woman who found a way to take control of her own life. She had lived as a concubine in the emperor's palace for several years without even meeting the emperor, and she may have felt bored, lonely, and resentful. When an opportunity came for her to step forward as a political offering to one of the Huns' rulers, she grabbed it. With her new husband, she traveled far away from her home—but her story still lives in China, where poets regarded her as a prudent, resolute woman who insisted on living her life as a human being rather than an imperial plaything. During the centuries of quiet, submissive women, Wan Zhaojun stands out, simply by volunteering to set the course of her own life. Her story has been told and retold by authors, playwrights, and artists, and she has come to *personify accord* between the different ethnic groups of China.

Not all outstanding Chinese women lived centuries ago. Cixi, the Dowager Empress, ruled China in the late nineteenth and early twentieth centuries. As a young girl, she married the emperor, but she was his lowest-ranking concubine. She had the good fortune, however, to give birth to the emperor's only

WOMEN IN THE WORLD OF CHINA

Wang Zhaojun

Cixi refused to confine herself to the "inside" world. Unlike many Chineese women today whose lives remain within their homes, Cixi was active in the male "outside" world.

son. This meant that when the emperor died, Cixi's six-year-old son took the throne. Cixi acted as *regent*.

Cixi used her power to revitalize China. She brought an end to the many rebellions that had been tearing apart China; she created schools for the study of foreign languages; she built Western-style arsenals; and she sought to end government corruption. But for all the good Cixi did for her country, she was also ruthless about holding on to her power. When her son grew up, took a wife, and had a baby, Cixi ordered that her little grandson be killed. Soon after, the young emperor and his wife also died mysteriously. Cixi then placed another nephew, a three-year-old child she had adopted, on the throne, making her once more the regent.

When her nephew grew up, Cixi at last retired from government. She could not bear to stand by, however, and watch while he fell under the influence of

WOMEN IN THE WORLD OF CHINA

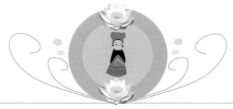

WOMAN'S WRITING

We do not know the names of all the outstanding women in China's history. For instance, long ago in the third century C.E. in a remote part of China, intelligent women created Nushu, a unique system of writing that has been used exclusively by women for centuries. Since girls were forbidden the privilege of learning to read and write, Nushu was developed in secrecy. Some characters were taken from Chinese, while others were invented, and all were rendered in a much more "cursive" style than written Chinese. It is a phonetic alphabet; its symbols represent sounds rather than ideas and pictures, as do Chinese ideograms. The graceful script was handed down from grandmother to granddaughter, from aunt to niece, from friend to friend—and it was never shared with men.

Today, only a handful of women can still read and write in Nushu. Says one ninety-eight-year-old woman, "The girls used to get together and sing and talk, and that's when we learned from one another. It made our lives better, because we could express ourselves that way."

The Imperial Palace, where Cixi once lived.

reformers who wanted to change China. When the more *conservative* government officials went to Cixi, asking for her help, Cixi returned to the throne. She placed her nephew under house arrest and supported the anti-foreign rebels.

During the *Boxer Rebellion* (see sidebar), however, foreigners overtook Beijing. Cixi and her *entourage* fled, only to return and accept the foreigners' peace terms. From then on, the imperial throne ruled in name only. In the last years of Cixi's life, she began to support the very reforms she had forbidden her nephew to make. On her deathbed, she still refused to let go of her power: she ordered that her adopted son be poisoned, and she placed another three-year-old boy on the emperor's throne. (This little boy, the last emperor of China, only ruled for three years before he was ousted.) On Cixi's deathbed, her final words were these: "Never again allow a woman to hold the supreme power in the State."

WOMEN IN THE WORLD OF CHINA

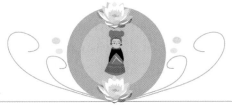

As the Chinese imperial government became weaker, European powers and America turned to a policy referred to as "carving up China's melon." In other words, each nation was scrambling to grab a piece of China for itself. The Russians got Port Arthur, the British got the New Territories around Hong Kong, and the Germans got a leasehold in Shantung.

The imperial court responded to this foreign threat by giving aid to various secret societies. The Empress Dowager believed that the secret societies might be the only way she could get rid of the Europeans. The Boxers, or "the Righteous and Harmonious Fists," were a religious society that had originally rebelled against the imperial government in Shantung in 1898. They practiced rituals and spells they believed made them impervious to bullets and pain. The Boxers also believed that the expulsion of "foreign devils" would magically renew Chinese society and begin a new golden age.

The Western response to the Boxer Rebellion was swift and severe. Within a couple months, an international force captured Beijing and forced the imperial government to agree to the most humiliating terms yet: the Boxer Protocol of 1901. Under this edict, European powers got the right to maintain military forces in the capital, thus placing the imperial government more or less under arrest.

The humiliation of the Boxer Protocols set China on a new course of reform. In 1901, the education system was reformed to allow the admission of girls, and the curriculum was changed from the study of the classics and Confucian studies to the study of Western mathematics, science, engineering, and geography. The Chinese began to send its young people to Europe and to Japan to study the new sciences, such as economics. Radical new Western ideas, such as Marxism, started making their way into China.

In many ways, Cixi's life seems to prove the Chinese proverb: "The fangs of the bamboo snake and the sting of the wasp are not as poisonous as a woman's heart." According to traditional Chinese thought, women who wield power have the potential to disrupt the social order and bring disaster. As Cixi lay dying, she apparently blamed her own womanhood for her many sins.

Cixi was indeed merciless and amoral when it came to protecting her power. She used all the skills she could lay her hands on, including manipulation, sabotage, and murder. As a woman, though, she was denied the weapons a man might have used. And in fact, she worked hard for her country in many ways. She was selfish—even evil—but she also proved that women can be as strong, as intelligent, and as courageous as any man.

In the twentieth century, Chinese women carried on the legacy of courage and strength they inherited from women like Mulan, Wu Zetian, Wang Zhaojun, and Cixi. Soong Ching-ling, wife of Dr. Sun Yat-sen, was a champion of social justice and women's liberation. Deng Yingchao was another outspoken advocate for women's rights. Ding Ling, a prominent writer, attacked the sexist attitudes of the Cultural Revolution.

Modern Chinese women continue to speak out on behalf of themselves and other Chinese women. For instance, Annette Lu is a prominent politician from the Republic of China (the island nation of Taiwan). On March 18, 2000, Lu was elected as the first female vice-president of the Republic of China, winning nearly 5 million votes. Mainland China (the People's Republic) does not view Lu positively. Beijing newspapers blasted her as being a "lunatic" and the "scum of the nation." Some of her own colleagues complain that she seems incapable of holding her tongue, behavior that severs her from the approved feminine stereotypes.

In the 1970s, Lu opened a coffee shop for women, a gathering place for the Taiwanese feminist movement. In 1979, she gave a speech that demanded

Cixi, the Dowager Empress

Modern Chinese women take their place in businesses beside men. A family-run business allows this woman to care for her child while working.

democracy in Taiwan and was charged with sedition (rebellion against the government). She was sentenced to twelve years in prison, but even captivity could not stop Lu; she wrote two novels on toilet paper before she was paroled five years later for health reasons. In 1992, she won a seat in Taiwan's legislature.

Sun Yat-sen is known as the "Father of the Revolution," because for over twenty years he struggled to bring a nationalist and democratic revolution to China. His idea of revolution was based on three principles: nationalism, democracy, and equalization. He died in 1924, with China in ruins, torn by the violence of competing warlords. His ideas, however, fueled the revolutionary fervor of the early twentieth century and became the basis of the Nationalist government established by Chiang Kai-shek in 1928.

While some Chinese women break into politics, others are excelling in the arts and in sports. Cobra, for example, is an all-female rock band that has startled Chinese society. One member of the band, Wang Xiaofang, was quoted in Details magazine: "This is not what traditional people do. Chinese people don't know what rock is. They don't know what kind of 'monsters' we are." Another courageous woman is Bai Jie, a soccer player who played with her team in the Woman's World Cup. Referred to as the "steel rose" and the "ghost killer," Bai's teammates call her "Sister Bai," a term of affection and respect that acknowledges the leadership role she plays. Women like these act as role models for other Chinese women. They demonstrate what is possible.

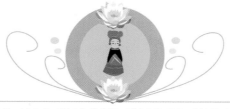

Taiwan is an island that lies close off Mainland China's west coast. Ever since the Chinese Communists founded the People's Republic of China on the mainland, the political status of Taiwan has been a controversial issue.

When the Qing Dynasty fell in 1911, the Republic of China governed Mainland China until 1949, when it was defeated by the communists. When Mao Tse-tung proclaimed the People's Republic of China, the Republic of China retreated to the island of Taiwan. Despite the actual political situation, the government of the Republic of China still claimed Mainland China, including Tibet and outer Mongolia.

In 1991, however, President Lee Teng-hui stated that the government will no longer challenge communist rule on the mainland. Current President Chen Shui-bian's position is that "Taiwan is an independent, sovereign country. . . . There is one country on each side of the Taiwan Strait." This means that Taiwan or the Republic of China is one country on one side of the Taiwan Strait and the People's Republic of China is a different country on the other side—instead of being two authorities within the same country of China. Although the government has stopped treating Mainland China as part of its territory, Taiwan's National Assembly has not formally renounced its jurisdiction over mainland China and outer Mongolia.

A Modern Chinese woman.

Throughout China's long history, outstanding women have proven that women are more than cattle, more than servants, more than the narrow roles men created for them. Today, in the twenty-first century, women continue to redefine what it means to be a Chinese woman. They are demonstrating that women have power, talent, and intelligence—and they will no longer be hidden away inside a man's house. Instead, they are ready to take their place as leaders and artists, politicians and scientists, authors and humanitarians. They are not only changing the shape of their own lives; they are also transforming Chinese culture. But they face many challenges.

"CHINESE WOMEN HAVE A HISTORY, BUT THEY HAVE A FUTURE TOO."
—XINRAN

6

UNBOUND LIVES:
MODERN CHANGE AND CHINESE WOMEN

Recently in China, a forty-three-year-old woman was laid off from a food-processing plant. She was desperate enough for work that she planned to interview for a part-time job cleaning windows at sixty cents an hour. "If you're over thirty-five, it's very hard to find work," she said. "What can you do? You have young and old ones to look after. You're too old to learn new skills. You're not attractive anymore. Nobody wants us."

A few years ago in Tianjin, a coastal manufacturing city of nine million people and a center of the Chinese textile industry, 320,000 people were laid off. Women were hit the hardest. Recently, China's Ministry of Labor reported that women accounted for only 39 percent of China's workforce but nearly 61 percent of its laid-off workers. Surveys show that 75 percent of laid-off women are still unemployed a year later, compared with fewer than 50 percent of the men who were laid off at the same time. These workers have often lost more than their jobs; they've also lost their right to medical care, child care, and funeral benefits.

A Chinese textile factory.

WOMEN IN THE WORLD OF CHINA

Some blame this reality on the arrival of *free-market capitalism* in China. As state-owned industries close or downsize, women over thirty-five are far more likely to be laid off and far less likely to find a new job than any other group in China. Companies are also reluctant to hire older women, since these women usually carry the responsibility of caring for their children as well as older parents.

China is not the same world it was a hundred years ago. Today, official laws encourage equal job opportunity for women. But laws cannot erase the centuries-old beliefs that still exist in the minds of many Chinese men. As a result, companies openly favor men over women for many types of work. One law school graduate looking for a job said many companies thought jobs were too strenuous for women if they involved travel or work in rural towns. "When they are willing to hire a woman," she said, "they want someone who's beautiful and capable, too."

Last year, in a Chinese city, laid-off workers scanned the newspapers' help-wanted listings. Many of the ads they saw read like this:

Secretary, Beijing resident, female, under 30, above 1.65 meters tall, must have regular features.

Promotion girl, female, under 28 years old, above 1.65 meters tall, white skin, skinny, healthy.

These actual ads from Chinese newspapers indicate what many employers are really looking for: a pretty girl to be their mistress. Even after the Cultural Revolution and all the changes brought by the twentieth century, too many twenty-first-century Chinese men still think of women just as their ancestors did: as inferior beings who exist for the convenience of men.

Desperate for work, many women agree to be men's "secretaries," although they are really mistresses. Others go even further and turn to prostitution. Fifty

The Chinese economy has many problems.

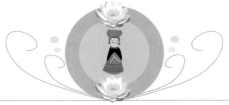

Some Chinese women are finding ways to handle unemployment and look out for each other at the same time. A recent article in **The Age** describes Mrs. Wang, a laid-off instrument maker in Tianjin who has started her own business creating trimmings for garments. She now employs one hundred workers, all women. Their pay is on a piecework basis—but they at least make more than they would if they were only receiving welfare payments. Mrs. Wang's business is one of a handful being supported by the Tianjin Women's Business Incubator, an organization that supplies new businesses for women with secretarial, administrative, and legal support, while also providing small loans. The project is being funded by the local government, the United Nations Development Program, and the Australian government.

years ago, under Mao's policies, prostitution virtually disappeared from China. Today, it is back, although under a different name—*san pei*, which means literally "three companies." Some say that the three kinds of company refer to chatting, drinking, and dancing with clients; others say it includes far more. These

businesses are most common in the rural areas of China. The Chinese police estimate that 4 million women in China are prostitutes. Another 18 million young women have no regular jobs; they roam around the country, supporting themselves however they can.

Chinese women who do not turn to prostitution may still see men as their "meal tickets." One college graduate interviewed by Shanghai's Women's Federation reported that finding a rich husband was the most important thing in her life. "Men always think themselves superior to women," she said, "and they like to provide comfortable living conditions for their children and spouses." Another college student who was surveyed said that finding a good man would be "like a reincarnation," since she did not want to depend on her own abilities to strive for a better life.

Women who manage to find financial success on their own often cannot find potential dates, let alone husbands. Chinese men tend to be put off by educated, self-confident women. In a recent *Washington Post* article, a director of a large matchmaking service in Beijing reported, "Men who are successful in their professions—it only takes us a few days to find them a match. The success rate is 100 percent. But women who are successful in their professions? It may take us a few years, if we ever find a match. The success rate is the lowest of anyone." The problem, the director says, is that Chinese men want women who are "young and pretty and gentle. They want wives who will look after the family." There is even a Chinese word for strong and capable women—*nuqiangren*. The word is used as an insult. "Everyone knows," the matchmaking service director said, "nuqiangren have unhappy family lives."

Chinese men don't want to "lose face" by having a wife that might be more educated or more successful than they are. They want a traditional, stable family, one where the woman takes care of the home and children. Meanwhile, some modern Chinese women are changing their views on the role of women.

Changing roles in China means that some men now share in child care and household responsibilities.

Although men can no longer have two wives, traditional attitudes still linger in modern China.

This discrepancy between the sexes makes for problems when it comes to marriage.

Women can't help but feel pressured to fall back into the old ways of thinking about themselves. After all, it's easy to absorb the prevailing attitudes in the society around you—especially when you are faced with a shaky economy where you may not be able to find a job. Just as long-ago Chinese women once went along with footbinding, today's women are often sucked backward into traditional attitudes about marriage and female inferiority. Even when women try to resist the stereotypes, they face an uphill road. Male prejudice affects Chinese women employed in both unskilled and professional jobs.

A recent French newspaper tells about a nurse in Shanghai who was fined for failing to wear lipstick. A colleague was also given a fine for having a hole in her stocking. "Whether or not I choose to wear lipstick is a private manner," the nurse wrote in a letter to the local newspaper. But the newspaper's male readers sided with the hospital, and an editorial was written, advising nurses to "spruce up" for their work. Hospital spokespeople defended the fines, saying that "seeing a pretty face cheers patients up."

In urban China, where people are exposed to media from around the world, viewpoints are gradually changing. But in the countryside, communities are often nearly as isolated as they were hundreds of years ago. Practices continue there that often seem *barbaric*.

For example, in *The Good Women of China*, Xinran includes a letter from a young boy with a "secret":

> It is not really a secret, because everyone in the village knows. There is an old, crippled man of sixty here who recently bought a wife. The girl looks very young—I think she must have been kidnapped. This happens a lot around here, but many of the girls escape later. The old man is afraid his wife will run off, so he has tied a thick iron chain around her. Her waist has been rubbed raw by the heavy chain. I think it will kill her.

In September 2000, the *Straits Times* reported on a similar story from Beijing. A ninety-member gang had kidnapped 240 women and sold them to farmers who were desperate for wives. (Many poor farmers are unable to find wives because they cannot afford to pay a dowry, and many women prefer to either marry a better-off man or move into a city to look for work.) The women, who ranged in age from sixteen to twenty-four, had been told that the kidnappers would find them jobs.

Sometimes it seems as though for every step forward that Chinese women take, their world shoves them two steps backward. China's troubled economy, its one-child policy, and its ancient heritage of *chauvinism*, all play a role in

REDUCING SUICIDE AMONG CHINESE WOMEN

The All-China Women's Federation, China's largest women's organization, has organized crisis hotlines and women's shelters to give women opportunities to discuss their problems and seek solutions. The Federation supports a national suicide prevention plan. "Suicide prevention is clearly a complex problem that needs to be addressed by the coordinated action of multiple government and non-governmental agencies," said a Federation representative.

In more ways than one, Chinese women travel a long, hard road.

Chinese women's lives. The pressure on them is enormous—and depression and suicide are growing problems. Suicide is particularly common among women in rural areas, where suicide rates are three times that of urban areas. China is the only country in the world where the number of female suicides exceeds the number of male suicides. Xie Lihua, a Chinese journalist, observes: "From their birth these women are being regarded as less important family members than their brothers. . . . they don't understand the value of their lives."

Although the picture we've drawn of women's lives in China is bleak, Chinese society continues to change rapidly. What was once a rural, farm-oriented society has become *urbanized* and industrialized. Standards of living have improved drastically, and the economy as a whole has become more prosperous. Before 1949, the *illiteracy* rate in China was 80 percent. Now, illiteracy has declined to less than seven percent (but more girls than boys still can't read). In the early twentieth century, the life expectancy of the Chinese people averaged thirty-five years; today, it is in the low seventies (eight years lower than that of the residents of developed countries but ten years higher than that of the residents of other developing countries).

All this means that in numerous ways, life is better for China's women. Many problems remain to be solved, however. As Westerners, it's easy to point our fingers at the injustices in Chinese society. A better approach might be to examine our own minds and traditions to see where we too are at fault. Prejudice and injustice are difficult sediments to strain from the world's sea of cultures and countries.

But the human spirit is strong. In *Beyond the Narrow Gate*, Leslie Chang includes this poem by Wen Yi-to:

So this ditch of hopeless dead winter
May well boast a certain splendor;
Then if the frogs can't bear the silence
Out of dead water a song will rise.

These little girls will encounter both challenges and opportunities.

Chang looks with hope toward women's future. "If our mothers were . . . valiantly continuing to sing in spite of their broken pasts," she writes, "then we, their [daughters have] reaped the rewards of that courage. Out of dead water a song will rise."

As China's women shake free from the bindings of the past, their song will grow ever stronger.

FURTHER READING

Chang, Leslie. *Beyond the Narrow Gate*. New York: Plume, 2000.

Ching, Pang-Mei Natasha. *Bound Feet and Western Dress*. New York: Anchor Books, 1997.

Ebrey, Patricia Buckley. *The Inner Quarters*. Berkeley: University of California Press, 1993.

Xinran. *The Good Women of China*. New York: Pantheon, 2002.

Yen Mah, Adeline. *Falling Leaves: The Memoir of an Unwanted Chinese Daughter*. New York: Broadway Books, 1997.

———. *Watching the Tree*. New York: Broadway Books, 2001.

Yung, Judy. *Unbound Voices*. Berkeley: University of California Press, 1999.

FOR MORE INFORMATION

All-China Women's Federation
www.women.org.cn/womenorg/English/english/international/

China and Women's History
womenshistory.about.com/od/china/

China's One-Child Policy
axe.acadiau.ca/~043638z/one-child/

Chinese Women's Issues
newton.uor.edu/Departments&Programs/AsianStudiesDept/china-
women.html

Cixi, the Dowager Empress
womenshistory.about.com/library/bio/blbio_cixi.htm

Iron Women: Chinese Propaganda Posters
www.iisg.nl/~landsberger/iron.html

The Historical Mulan
www.colorq.org/Articles/2000/realMulan.htm

Women in China: Past and Present
acc6.its.brooklyn.cuny.edu/ ~phalsall/texts/chinwomn.html

Women's Issues
womensissues.about.com/

Women Watch
www.un.org/womenwatch/

The World of Nushu
www2.ttcn.ne.jp/~orie/home.htm

Publisher's note:
The Web sites listed on these pages were active at the time of publication. The
publisher is not responsible for Web sites that have changed their addresses or
discontinued operation since the date of publication. The publisher will review
and update the Web sites upon each reprint.

GLOSSARY

accentuate To accent; emphasize.

accord A formal agreement.

activists People who act in support of something.

barbaric Savage

bourgeois Relating to the middle class.

chauvinism Undue partiality to a group or place.

classical Traditional; enduring.

collective A number of persons or things that are considered to be and treated as a single unit.

communists People who believe in the theory that goods should be owned in common and available for use by all.

concubine A woman with whom a man lives without being married; in some cultures she has social status, although it is below that of a wife.

conservative Wants to maintain a traditional way of life rather than change.

controversial Likely to cause disagreement.

creeds A set of fundamental beliefs.

demarcation A point of separation.

dictatorship A form of government in which the power rests with one person or a very small group of people.

egalitarian Having the characteristic of human equality.

egomaniac Someone who is concerned with only his or her own activities or needs.

entourage One's attendants or associates.

epitaph A brief statement honoring someone, often on their tombstone.

eroding Wearing away.

exploitation The act of using someone or something for one's own advantage.

feminists People who believe that women should have the same rights and opportunities as men.

free-market capitalism An economic system in which competition is the driving force behind making money.

ideals Standards of perfection or excellence.

illiteracy The condition of not being able to read or write.

imperial dynasty Rule by an emperor.

individualism Doctrine putting the interests of the individual first.

infanticide The killing of an infant.

internalize To keep within oneself as a guiding principle.

IUD Intrauterine device. A device implanted in the uterus to prevent pregnancy.

looted Plundered.

Opium War A war between Britain and China over the British smuggling of opium into China. China lost, and one of the results was the turning over of Hong Kong to Great Britain.

regent One who governs a kingdom when the ruler cannot, usually because he or she is too young.

republic A government in which power is held by a body of citizens entitled to vote.

status quo The way things presently are.

sterilized Made incapable of reproducing.

subordinate An inferior; lacking importance.

theocratic Relating to rule by someone believed to be divinely guided.

urbanized Took on the characteristics of a city.

INDEX

PICTURE CREDITS

BIOGRAPHIES

Ellyn Sanna is the author of nearly a hundred fiction and nonfiction books for both children and adults. She has written several adult books on women's issues. Her experience parenting three children while also working as a full-time editor has given her firsthand experience at juggling some of women's conflicting roles.

Dr. Mary Jo Dudley is the director of Cornell University's Gender and Global Change Department, which focuses on the evolving role of gender around the world. She is also the associate director of Latin American Studies at Cornell.